ATLAS and GLOBE SKILLS

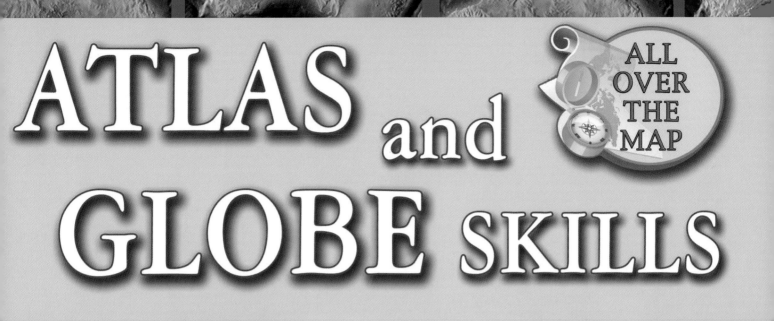

ALL OVER THE MAP

Ellen Rodger

Crabtree Publishing Company

www.crabtreebooks.com

Crabtree Publishing Company

www.crabtreebooks.com

Author: Ellen Rodger
Publishing plan research and development:
   Sean Charlebois, Reagan Miller
   Crabtree Publishing Company
Series editor: Valerie J. Weber
Editors: Valerie J. Weber, Crystal Sikkens
Proofreaders: Barbara Kiely Miller, Kelly McNiven,
   Shannon Welbourn
Editorial director: Kathy Middleton
Project manager: Summit Kumar (Q2A Bill Smith)
Art direction: Joita Das (Q2A Bill Smith)
Design: Roshan (Q2A Bill Smith)
Cover design: Ken Wright
Photo research: Ranjana Batra (Q2A Bill Smith),
   Crystal Sikkens
Production coordinator and prepress technician:
   Katherine Berti
Print coordinators: Katherine Berti, Margaret Amy Salter

Photographs:
Cover: Photowitch/Dreamstime (boy), other images by Shutterstock; P1: Dragon Images/ Shutterstock; P4: Pressmaster/Shutterstock; P5: Universal Images Group Limited/ Alamy(tl); P5: Tomboy2290/Dreamstime (br); P6 & 7: numb/Alamy; P7: STOCK4B Creative/Getty Images; P8: David Maska/Shutterstock; P9: Fotolia (t), Dreamstime (b); P10: John Foxx/Stockbyte/Getty Images; P11: DonSmith/ Alamy; P12: moodboard/Moodboard Premium/Glow Images; P13: Sailorr/Shutterstock; P14: Pakhnyushcha/Shutterstock; P15: Mickael David/Author's Image Ltd/Alamy; P16: kak2s/Shutterstock; P17: Djexplo/Wikipedia(t); P17: Sue Flood/Oxford Scientific/Getty Images(b); P18: Leremy/Shutterstock; P19: Nationalatlas.gov; P21: Cia.gov; P22: Taylor Jackson/Shutterstock; P23: oblong1/ Shutterstock(br), ruzanna/Shutterstock (bl); P24: Pressmaster/Shutterstock; P25: Nationalatlas.gov; P26: Stuwdamdorp/Alamy; P28: De Agostini/DEA PICTURE LIBRARY/Getty Images; P29: SSPL/Getty Images(tl); P29: jimmi/ Shutterstock(cr); P29: David R. Frazier Photolibrary, Inc./Alamy(bl); P30: asiseeit/ iStockphoto; P31: Sam Bloomberg-Rissman/Blend RM/Glow Images

Q2A Art Bank: P20, 23 (tl), 27

t=top, tr=top right, tl=top left, bl= bottom left, br=bottom right, b=bottom

Library and Archives Canada Cataloguing in Publication

Rodger, Ellen
      Atlas and globe skills / Ellen Rodger.

(All over the map)
Includes index.
Issued also in electronic format.
ISBN 978-0-7787-4490-0 (bound).--ISBN 978-0-7787-4495-5 (pbk.)

      1. Atlases--History--Juvenile literature. 2. Globes--Juvenile literature. I. Title. II. Series: All over the map (St. Catharines, Ont.)

G1021.R63 2013   j912   C2012-908249-X

Library of Congress Cataloging-in-Publication Data

Rodger, Ellen.
  Atlas and globe skills / Ellen Rodger.
         pages cm. -- (All over the map)
  Includes index.
  ISBN 978-0-7787-4490-0 (reinforced library binding) -- ISBN 978-0-7787-4495-5 (pbk.) -- ISBN 978-1-4271-9328-5 (electronic (pdf)) -- ISBN 978-1-4271-9316-2 (electronic (html))
  1. Maps--Juvenile literature. 2. Atlases--Juvenile literature. 3. Globes--Juvenile literature. I. Title.
  GA105.6.R624 2013
  912.01'4--dc23
                                          2012048488

Crabtree Publishing Company

www.crabtreebooks.com   1-800-387-7650

Printed in the USA/052013/JA20130412

Published in Canada
Crabtree Publishing
616 Welland Ave.
St. Catharines, ON
L2M 5V6

Published in the United States
Crabtree Publishing
PMB 59051
350 Fifth Avenue, 59th Floor
New York, New York 10118

Published in the United Kingdom
Crabtree Publishing
Maritime House
Basin Road North, Hove
BN41 1WR

Published in Australia
Crabtree Publishing
3 Charles Street
Coburg North
VIC, 3058

CONTENTS

Atlases, Globes, and Geography   4

What is an Atlas?   6

What is a Globe?   8

Atlas Features   10

Globe Features   12

Reading Atlases and Globes   14

Dividing Up the Planet   16

Symbols and Colors   18

Scale and Distance   20

Grids and Projections   22

The World around Us   24

Countries and Culture   26

The Changing World   28

Use Your Skills   30

Glossary and Index   32

Atlases, Globes, and Geography

People use globes and atlases everyday. These tools show us how and where people live. They also show physical and human-made features of Earth. Physical features include mountains, oceans, and lakes. Human-made features include country borders, cities, and roads.

▲ *Globes are great tools for exploring and learning about the world!*

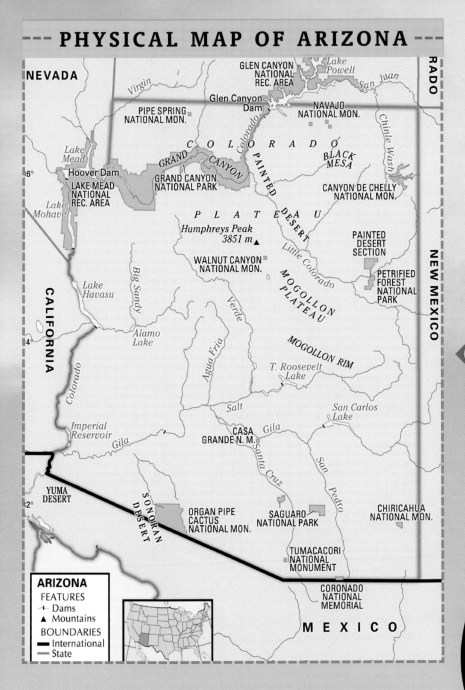

PHYSICAL MAP OF ARIZONA

NEVADA

Virgin

GLEN CANYON NATIONAL REC. AREA

Lake Powell

San Juan

RADO

Glen Canyon Dam

PIPE SPRING NATIONAL MON.

NAVAJO NATIONAL MON.

Chinle Wash

C O L O R A D O

Lake Mead

Hoover Dam

16°

LAKE MEAD NATIONAL REC. AREA

GRAND CANYON

GRAND CANYON NATIONAL PARK

Colorado

BLACK MESA

P A I N T E D   D E S E R T

CANYON DE CHELLY NATIONAL MON.

NEW MEXICO

Lake Mohave

P L A T E A U

Humphreys Peak 3851 m ▲

WALNUT CANYON NATIONAL MON.

Little Colorado

PAINTED DESERT SECTION

CALIFORNIA

Lake Havasu

Big Sandy

Verde

M O G O L L O N   P L A T E A U

PETRIFIED FOREST NATIONAL PARK

4°

Alamo Lake

Agua Fria

M O G O L L O N   R I M

T. Roosevelt Lake

Colorado

Salt

San Carlos Lake

Imperial Reservoir

Gila

CASA GRANDE N. M.

Gila

Santa Cruz

San Pedro

2°

YUMA DESERT

S O N O R A N   D E S E R T

ORGAN PIPE CACTUS NATIONAL MON.

SAGUARO NATIONAL PARK

CHIRICAHUA NATIONAL MON.

TUMACACORI NATIONAL MONUMENT

CORONADO NATIONAL MEMORIAL

M E X I C O

ARIZONA

FEATURES
- ⊣ Dams
- ▲ Mountains

BOUNDARIES
- ▬ International
- ▬ State

Globes and atlases help us understand **geography**. Geography is the study of Earth's **landscapes**, plants, animals, and people. Landscapes consist of all the natural features of an area, such as rivers and mountains. Features made by people, such as roads and buildings, are part of landscapes as well.

◀ *This map shows the physical features of Arizona in the United States. It can be found in an atlas.*

▼ *The globe below shows you where the United States is located in the world.*

How people live has a lot to do with where they live. Imagine you lived in Hawaii where the weather was warm. You would not need winter boots! A globe will show Hawaii's location in the world. It can show you why it has a warm **climate**. An atlas will show maps of Hawaii. These maps will give information as to where the people of Hawaii live or what foods are grown there.

What is an Atlas?

An atlas is a book of maps. A **map** is a drawing of an area of land. It is usually a flat, **two-dimensional** (2-D) drawing. It shows the size and shape of an area. We see the area as if we were far above it.

▼ *This atlas map shows roads and highways in London, England.*

Atlases and their maps give information about many places. Some maps tell us about a physical place, such as a city or a country. Others tell us about the people who live in a place. They can show us what areas of a country people live in and what languages they speak.

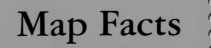

Some atlases are made just for children.

Map Facts

The word "atlas" was first used by mapmaker Gerardus Mercator in 1595 to describe his collection of maps.

What is a Globe?

A globe is a **sphere**, or round ball, designed to look like Earth.
In fact, a globe is a **scale model** of Earth. A scale model is a
copy of something. It is much smaller than the original.

▲ Globes can be huge, like these in an old library.

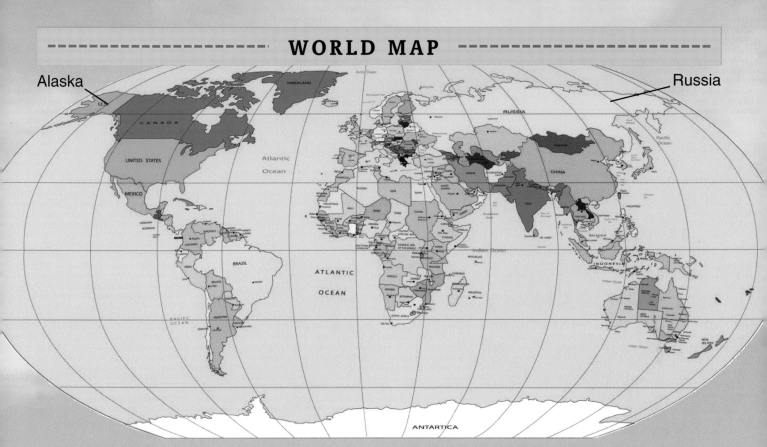

Alaska

Russia

A map is flat. It uses only two dimensions—length and width. However, globes are round and **three-dimensional** (3-D). They show length, width, and depth. On some flat maps, **continents** may appear larger than they really are when compared to other continents. Globes make them appear the correct size in **proportion** to the other continents.

Globes show you the actual distances countries or continents are from one another. For example, on the world map above, Alaska, which is part of the United States, looks very far away from Russia. However, on the globe, you can see they are actually quite close.

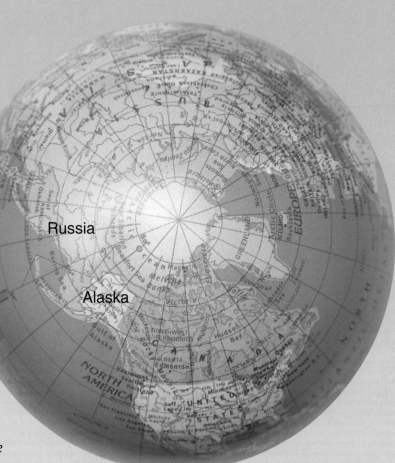

Russia

Alaska

Atlas Features

Atlases contain a lot of helpful information about different countries. If you were looking for the cities in Brazil, a map in an atlas could help! But, how would you find it?

Atlases have common parts to help readers find information they are looking for. A table of contents is found at the beginning of an atlas. It lists everything that appears in the book.

Most atlases also have instructions on how to read a map and information on the many different kinds of maps shown in it.

You can find out a lot about the world from the different maps in an atlas!

The index is an important feature in an atlas. It is found at the back of the book. Place names are listed in alphabetical order. Beside each place is a page number. That page number is where you can find a map that contains the place you are looking for in the atlas. Beside the page number is a letter and number. These are called **grid references**. These **coordinates** will show you the exact location of your place on the map.

▲ *Some atlases also have landforms listed in the index, such as mountains, rivers, or lakes.*

Globe Features

Globes are perfect models of Earth. They are a sphere and spin like Earth does. Globes are tilted, too. The tilt shows Earth's axis. The axis is an **imaginary** line between the North Pole and the South Pole. Earth spins on its axis.

Like maps, there are different kinds of globes. There are globes that show the physical features of Earth, such as mountains, hills, and deserts. Some of these globes have raised areas to better show where mountains and hills are.

This globe shows the physical features of Earth. You might have one like this in your classroom.

Other globes show the political features of Earth. These globes show the borders of the continents and countries around the world. Each country is a different color.

All globes show Earth's oceans and many of the world's lakes and rivers.

▲ *This photo taken from space shows how Earth curves in a sphere.*

Reading Atlases and Globes

It might seem simple to read an atlas or a globe. After all, they just show pictures, right? Not quite. The information in an atlas or on a globe can be hard to understand. You have to know something about geography.

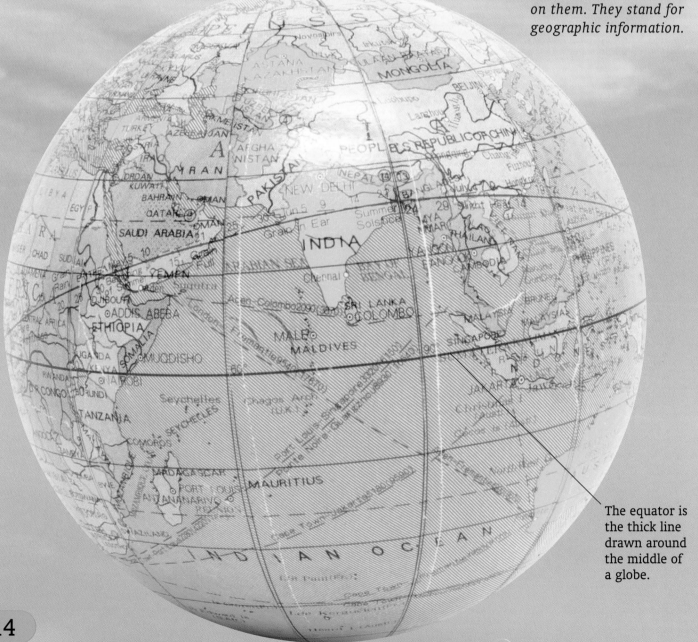

▼ *Globes have many lines on them. They stand for geographic information.*

The equator is the thick line drawn around the middle of a globe.

All globes and atlas maps have lines on them. These lines are called **reference** lines. Reference lines do not actually appear on our planet. They are imaginary. They help us figure out distances and where something is located.

Reference lines include the **equator**, the **prime meridian**, **latitude lines**, and **longitude lines**. These lines divide Earth into sections so we can easily find places.

Map Facts

The equator reference line divides Earth into two parts. The top half is called the **Northern Hemisphere**. It lies above the equator. The bottom half is called the **Southern Hemisphere**. It stretches below the equator.

This young man is sitting on the equator in Ecuador, South America! You can follow the equator reference line on a globe to find other continents and countries the equator runs through.

Dividing Up the Planet

Atlas maps and globes must follow a basic standard, set up thousands of years ago. Long ago, the Greeks divided a globe-like circle into 360 sections. These sections were called degrees. We use the latitude and longitude reference lines to mark these degrees on a globe or map. These lines help us locate places on Earth.

Tthe equator and prime meridian are both at 0º. Latitude and longitude lines start from these reference lines.

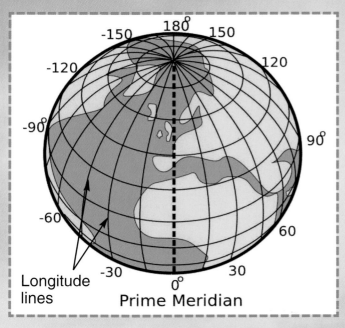

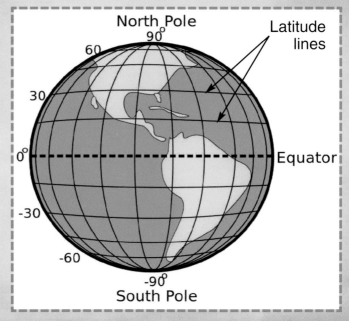

▲ Because Earth is a sphere, the lines of longitude meet at the North and South Poles. The space between the longitude lines gets wider as the lines get closer to the equator.

▲ Lines of latitude get shorter as they get closer to the North and South Pole.

Longitude lines run vertically, or up and down, Earth. They measure the distance of any point on Earth from the prime meridian. The prime meridian is at 0°. The lines run 180° to the east and 180° to the west. **Latitude lines** run horizontally, or around or across, Earth. They measure the distance of a point in degrees from the equator. The equator is at 0°. These lines run 90° to the north and 90° to the south.

▼ The Geographic North Pole is at 90°N. This is where Earth's axis meets its surface. It is the northernmost point on Earth.

Symbols and Colors

Globes and atlases use a common system, or language, for giving information. This language is made up of symbols. The symbols stand for real places and real landforms. These symbols are explained in a box called a key or a legend.

▼ *Without a legend or key, it would be difficult to find **landmarks** on a map.*

COMPLETE MAP TOOLKIT AND LEGEND

HIGHWAY	BUS STATION	POLICE STATION	SWIMMING POOL
MAJOR ROAD	TAXI STAND	FIRE STATION	FAST FOOD
SECONDARY ROAD	LIGHT RAIL STATION	HOSPITAL	FOOD COURT
RIVER	TRAIN STATION	LIBRARY	CINEMA
PROPOSED ROAD	AIRPORT	POST OFFICE	PUBLIC TOILET
BRIDGE	SEAPORT	EMBASSY	TELEPHONE
TOLL	APARTMENT	SHOPPING MALL	PETROL STATION
TRAFFIC LIGHT	FACTORY	HOTEL	RESTING AREA
ONE WAY	MUSEUM	PLACE OF INTEREST	GOLF COURSE
HOUSING WITH NUMBER BESIDE ROAD	CHURCH	INFORMATION KIOSK	PLAYGROUND
LIGHT RAIL & STATION	CHINESE TEMPLE	HIGH COURT	NUCLEAR REACTOR
TRAIN RAIL & STATION	MOSQUE	PARKING AREA	
STATE BOUNDARY	HINDU TEMPLE		
CITY BOUNDARY	SCHOOL		
GRASS FIELD	COMMUNITY HALL		
SEA			
FOREST			

18

Some symbols are simple. They show a smaller version of the real thing. For example, a tiny tree may stand for a forest.

Atlases contain many different kinds of maps. It is important to read the legend to understand the map.

Some globes and atlas maps use different colors to show information, such as climate zones, temperature, or populations. The legend will let you know what each color stands for.

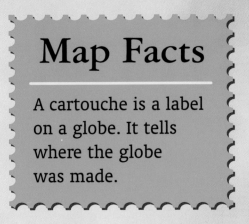

Map Facts

A cartouche is a label on a globe. It tells where the globe was made.

▼ *Look at the map below. Which states have temperatures over 85º fahrenheit?*

-MAXIMUM TEMPERATURES IN THE UNITED STATES-

LEGEND
(degrees Fahrenheit)

- more than 85.0
- 80.1–85.0
- 75.1–80.0
- 70.1–75.0
- 65.1–70.0
- 60.1–65.0
- 50.1–60.0
- 40.1–50.0
- less than 40.1

Data from the National Environmental Satellite, Data, and Information Service

Scale and Distance

Scale is the ratio, or proportion, between a distance on a map and the same distance on the ground. The scale on a map shows how much an area has been reduced. A **linear scale** uses a bar to show scale. The measurement of the bar represents a certain distance on land.

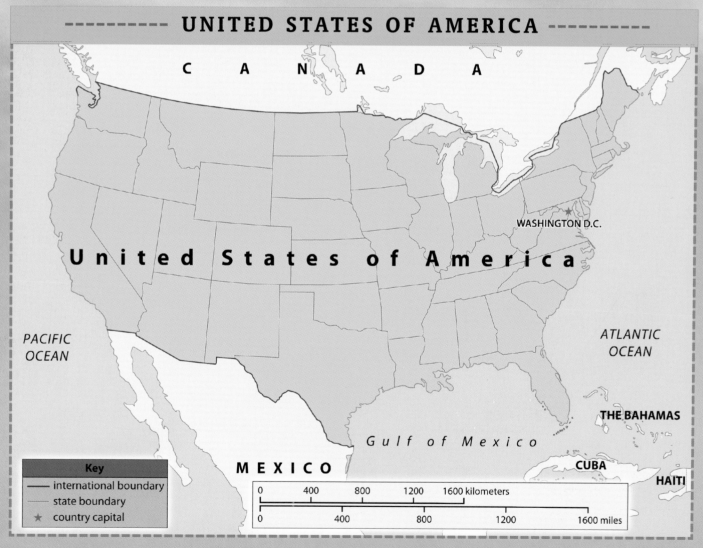

UNITED STATES OF AMERICA

CANADA

WASHINGTON D.C.

United States of America

PACIFIC OCEAN

ATLANTIC OCEAN

THE BAHAMAS

Gulf of Mexico

MEXICO

CUBA

HAITI

Key
—— international boundary
—— state boundary
★ country capital

0   400   800   1200   1600 kilometers

0   400   800   1200   1600 miles

▲ *Use a ruler to measure a section of this linear scale. Then place the ruler on the map. See if you can find out about how many miles or kilometers the United States is from the Pacific Ocean to the Atlantic Ocean.*

20

A ratio scale uses numbers to show scale. Ratio scales are shown like: 1:10,000. The "1" represents one unit of measurement on a map, often in inches or centimeters. The "10,000" represents the distance on land in that same unit. So, 1:10,000 means 1 inch on the map represents 10,000 inches on land.

Map Facts

Maps can be large-scale or small-scale. A large-scale map shows a small area in great detail, such as the streets of a city. A small-scale map shows a larger area in less detail, such as a country.

UNITED STATES OF AMERICA

State capital
Scale 1:27,000,000
Albers Equal-Area Projection
standard parallels 28°30'N and 45°30'N

500 Kilometers
0
0   500 Miles

▲ *This map shows both a linear scale and a ratio scale.*

Grids and Projections

Grids are the horizontal and vertical lines on a map. They divide the map into equal squares. Grids are labeled with numbers and letters at the top or bottom and side of a map. These labels are called grid references. They allow map readers to find an exact location.

Many atlases explain how to find a place using grid references. Imagine you want to find a place in an atlas. First, you must go to the index at the back of the atlas. Then, look up the place's name. You will find the page number of the correct map. Often the page number is bolded. You will also see the place's grid references. You can trace the grid references down and across the map to find the place.

▼ *Look at the atlas index below. What are the grid references for Alturas, CA?*

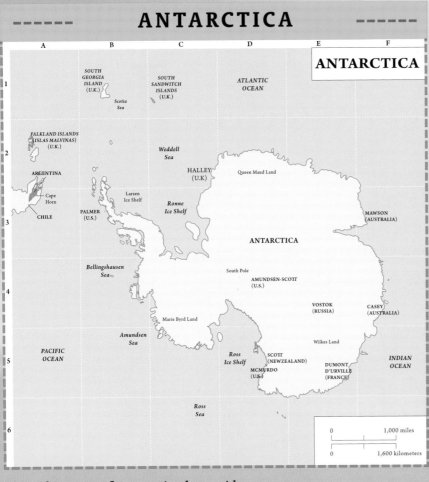

ANTARCTICA

	A	B	C	D	E	F

ANTARCTICA

SOUTH GEORGIA ISLAND (U.K.)
SOUTH SANDWITCH ISLANDS (U.K.)
ATLANTIC OCEAN
Scotia Sea
FALKLAND ISLANDS (ISLAS MALVINAS) (U.K.)
Weddell Sea
ARGENTINA
HALLEY (U.K)
Queen Maud Land
Cape Horn
Larsen Ice Shelf
Ronne Ice Shelf
CHILE
PALMER (U.S.)
MAWSON (AUSTRALIA)
ANTARCTICA
Bellingshausen Sea
South Pole
AMUNDSEN-SCOTT (U.S.)
VOSTOK (RUSSIA)
CASEY (AUSTRALIA)
Marie Byrd Land
Amundsen Sea
Wilkes Land
PACIFIC OCEAN
Ross Ice Shelf
SCOTT (NEWZEALAND)
MCMURDO (U.S.)
DUMONT D'URVILLE (FRANCE)
INDIAN OCEAN
Ross Sea

| 0 | 1,000 miles |
| 0 | 1,600 kilometers |

▲ *This map of Antarctica has grid references for finding locations. What can you find in square D2?*

Compare the size of North America on the globe to North America on the map. Can you see how much bigger North America seems to be on the map?

All maps are **projections**. They show a flat, two-dimensional (2-D) image of a round, three-dimensional (3-D) Earth. This transfer from 3-D to 2-D results in some changes. A continent's shape, area, or distance from another continent may not be accurate. This is why some countries sometimes appear huge on a flat map.

– NORTH AND SOUTH AMERICA –

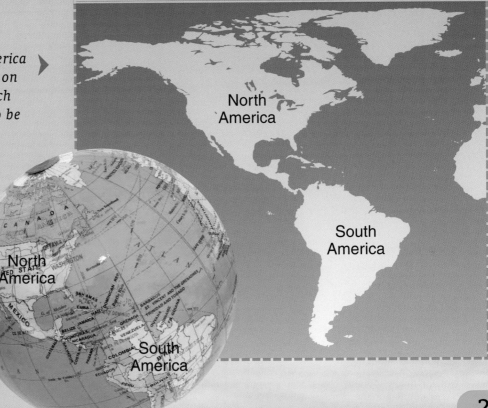

North America

South America

North America

South America

The World around Us

Globes are sometimes called the only true world map. This is because they show the real locations of every continent and country. It is easy to see how far Australia is from North America when you spin a globe.

▼ *A globe always shows a map of the whole world.*

Atlases break the world up into sections. Each section may contain maps of a continent and then the countries of that continent. Some atlases are thematic. This means the maps have a subject. Subjects can include the weather or population of a country. A population map will show the number of people living in a country.

Atlases and globes also provide information about the physical world around us. Physical maps show the features of an area. These features include rivers, lakes, mountains, or plains. These maps use specific colors to point out these physical features.

This thematic map shows the annual precipitation in California. Different colors show the amounts in inches.

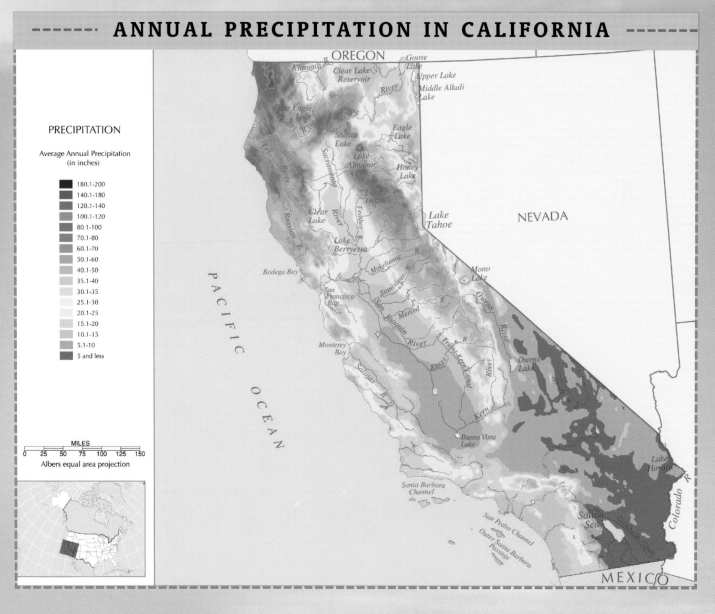

ANNUAL PRECIPITATION IN CALIFORNIA

PRECIPITATION

Average Annual Precipitation
(in inches)

- 180.1-200
- 140.1-180
- 120.1-140
- 100.1-120
- 80.1-100
- 70.1-80
- 60.1-70
- 50.1-60
- 40.1-50
- 35.1-40
- 30.1-35
- 25.1-30
- 20.1-25
- 15.1-20
- 10.1-15
- 5.1-10
- 5 and less

MILES
0   25   50   75   100   125   150
Albers equal area projection

Countries and Culture

Atlases and globes also show political boundaries. **Political boundaries** are the borders of countries, states, and provinces.

Political maps use the same mapping rules as other maps. Most also use different colors to define countries. What makes political maps interesting is how often they change. If you looked at a globe or atlas created in 1990, you would find many countries or states that no longer exist.

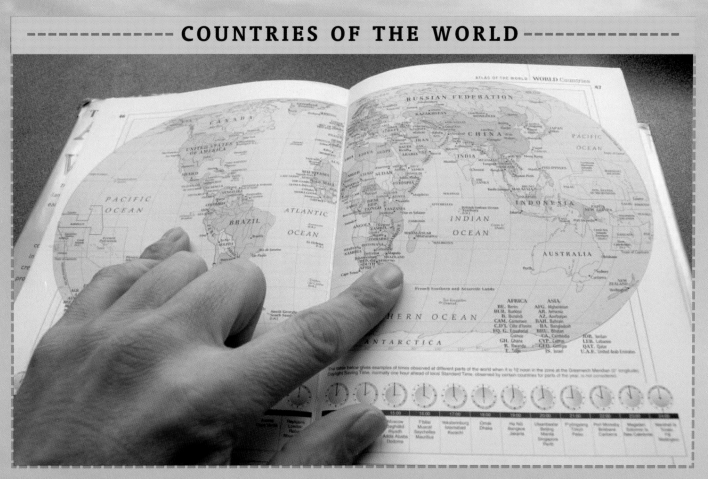

------------ COUNTRIES OF THE WORLD ------------

▲ *Look at how many countries there are in the world! It is easy to see when a map uses color to identify countries.*

U.S.S.R.

The Union of Soviet Socialist Republics (USSR) was shown on maps starting in 1922. In 1991, the USSR broke up. Today, that area appears on maps as a number of different countries.

AFTER 1991

Estonia
Latvia
Lithuania
Belarus
Moldova
Ukraine

Russia

Kazakhstan

Georgia Armenia Azerbaijan Uzbekistan Tajikistan Kyrgyzstan

Turkmenistan

Atlases contain information on people living in a country. A land use map will show how many people live in cities and how many in the country. The atlas may also explain where the areas are that most people work.

27

The Changing World

People have used maps and globes to describe the world for thousands of years. The earliest known atlas dates back to 150 A.D. The ancient Greeks made globes, but none are known to still exist.

The oldest existing geographic globe is called the Erdapfel. It was created by Martin Behaim from Germany in 1492. It was made before North America, South America, Australia, and Antarctica were discovered. Therefore, it does not show those continents.

▼ *Early atlas maps were often made by people who guessed at location and size. The maps looked nice, but were not correct.*

Early atlases contained maps that often did not reflect real life. Some showed made-up lands with imaginary creatures. They were drawn by hand. Over time, map and globe making became more correct. Today, maps are created on computers. Mapmakers now have a number of different sources for mapping information.

◄ *Celestial globes* are three-dimensional maps of the stars. Greek astronomers made them long ago. They show the position of stars in the sky. This globe was made in the 1530s.

▲
◄ *Mapmakers today use everything from photographs taken from airplanes to images of Earth taken from space.*

Use Your Skills

Finding information about a country or area can be exciting. Play this globe game to improve your research skills.

Close your eyes and spin a globe. Stop the globe by placing your index finger on a spot. Open your eyes and record some information about where you placed your finger.

1. If the spot has a name, write it down in a notebook.

2. Mark the nearest ocean and country. If you have picked a spot in the middle of the ocean, note its location.

▲ *You can learn a lot about the world by just spinning a globe.*

3. Write down the nearest lines of latitude and longitude. They will be the blue lines closest to your location.

▲ *Have you learned anything interesting about the world from playing the globe game?*

4. Find the equator on the globe. Is your spot below or above the equator?

After you have recorded your basic information, use an atlas to find your location. Does it provide more information? Can you tell a story about your location? Do people live there? What is it like?

Glossary

Note: Some boldfaced words are defined where they appear in the book.

climate The usual weather that occurs over time in an area

continents The seven major landmasses of the world

coordinates Numbers used to identify a place on a map

grid references Used to identify or find a place on a map

imaginary Not real, pretend

landmarks Physical features or human-made objects, such as monuments, that identify a certain area

prime meridian An imaginary line of zero longitude

projections Images that are copied or transferred onto something else

proportion A measurement of how one thing relates to another with regard to size, number, or amount

reference A source of information to determine something

three-dimensional Describes something that is not flat. Three-dimensional images can be viewed for length, width, and depth.

two-dimensional Describes something that is flat. A two-dimensional object has length and width, but no depth.

Index

celestial globes 29

color 13, 18, 19, 25, 26, 28

degrees 16, 17

equator 15, 16, 17, 31

Erdapfel 28

geography 4, 5, 14

Greeks 16, 28, 29

grid references 11, 22, 23

index 11, 22

latitude lines 15, 16, 17, 31

legend 18, 19

longitude lines 15, 16, 17, 31

physical maps 5, 12, 25

political boundaries 13, 26

prime meridian 15, 16, 17

reference lines 15, 16, 17

scale 20–21

symbols 18–19

table of contents 10

thematic maps 25

three-dimensional 9, 23, 29

two-dimensional 6, 23